NOW YOU KNOW

YOUR BEST SELF

ANSHUMAN SHARMA

To my beautiful daughters Gunn, Kli and my lovely wife Nilam

Contents

Contents

Contents

Contents

Contents

Preface

The purpose of writing this book is to create a manual for those who are looking forward to a resource to transform themselves. Most of the time we know about the right actions but we are so hard pressed with time that initiation is not taken. The power to create that meaningful change is inside all of us and we need a tender support and guidance to have meaningful and prosperous life. This resource would help all those who are seeking this transformation and desire to have a lasting positive change in life.

The process of true transformation is gradual and slow, it cannot be done instantly. Any immediate change cannot be true and durable. Transformation is not a one-step process but a series of steps understood and experienced within a proper time frame. The way of implementing these transformative ideas would be different for each individual and can only be understood and designed with experience. Reading can only help you to appreciate it but to bring an enduring positive change you need to execute and experience its power in your life. Real change would come from the output you will get by the end of each week.

All ideas presented in this work will not have equal effect on all readers; some ideas may work well on some individuals in comparison to others, certain ideas may not be applicable for few readers who may redesign it in their own context. A complete sincerity towards this transformation process would be the most important tool to gain the true benefits of this journey. By taking it casually you would only improve your knowledge about the success principles of your life, which if shared, could improve the life of someone else. This is not a magic pill which can make you a star in a day or even in a month, rather it is a gradual process to take the complete control of your life by making small positive changes every week and create a complete new you.

This is a journey of 52 weeks, which is exactly one year. We will take each step every weekend, understand the concept for the week and identify the ways to implement it in your life. You will implement the idea for the whole week i.e. Monday to Saturday (Week 1) and move on to the next idea again on Sunday and implement it on Week 2. It will not affect your daily life but will give you a strong but simple tool to excel your life both at work and in personal life. Once you complete a week you will be able to understand the concept in proper way and even experience it. You would be able to find ideas to integrate it in your life. It would be helpful if you could keep reminding yourself, regularly, about all the learning of previous weeks for each of remaining weeks. All 52 steps are designed in such a way that it would gel easily with your life, body, mind, emotions and soul. It would be great if you can give complete sincerity to these steps without any break as each would give strength to other. It is like a medicine course which would be effective if done according to prescription plan.

The ideas are simple and most of them would be known to readers, but somehow they were not implemented in their life for one reason or other. Readers can implement it according to the ways specified in the book or design their own methods, the purpose is to experience the power of the idea and try to make it a part of your life. All these ideas would cover almost every aspect in your life and would be enough to transform your life to give you more happiness, satisfaction, success and prosperity.

It is suggested that you should ease the intensity of implementation of an idea or altogether drop that particular method, if you feel uncomfortable in execution. You can come back to it later. The objective is to add value in your life not to make you uncomfortable.

CHAPTER ONE

WEEK ONE – Learn to say 'No'

'No' is one of the mantra for clarity and happiness. Many times we get engaged with those tasks and actions which should have never been started, which lead to pain, suffering and failure. This happens when we are not clear about ourselves, has hesitation, shyness or hitch. If we could learn to say 'No' to things which we do not want to do, that would save us from unnecessary suffering. 'No' should be a clear and decent rejection of unwanted offer, proposal or idea proposed to you. This does not mean to insult, appall or harm the other person, but plainly refusing your involvement in the task. This also does not mean to say 'No' to anything & everything and become a 'no person', but to be clear about the things which emotionally and logically do not suit you and would give you pain and discomfort.

There are several nice ways to say no. People sometimes use humor to reject something or cite some simple reasons for non-involvement or simply but firmly saying 'No' with a smiling face.

It would be great to have more clarity and self-belief in life to be a person with firm decisions.

Action Step

Action Step

This week, learn to say 'No'. Commit not to take any task or do anything which will bother you or put you at discomfort. Be very clear about the things which you would never do and would be refused. Write them down now.

CHAPTER TWO

WEEK TWO - Look in the eye of your fears

Every human being has fears, which resist them to do certain tasks. Fears give pain, therefore, we refuse to face them or even think about them. With time, these fears get more and more strength and their interference in our life increases. They will not go until faced and killed. If you face your fears, it would weaken their intensity and ultimately eliminate them from your life. This does not mean to do any illogical, illegal or immoral tasks, like if someone is afraid of water then she should not jump into deep water without learning swimming or if someone is afraid of snakes she goes to jungle and catch a poisonous snake without precautions. You need to prepare yourself to face your fears. If done the right way this fear will vanish from your life. If you are afraid of public speaking then you must practice well and find smaller opportunities to present and improve then move on to bigger challenges.

Facing the fear makes our heart beat faster making uncomfortable. This is also a nice way to know about your fears, anything giving you unease maybe one of your fear. You can eliminate your fear by taking it head-on with thorough preparation. If you have fear of driving, then learn it well from an expert and drive on crowded roads, daily.

Fears are the major obstacle to happiness and fulfillment in our lives, more they lose strength happier we become. This would be clearly visible to you by the end of the week.

Action Step

This week we will face two of our fears. Identify two of them, maybe small ones, and write them down. Plan for the steps to be taken to face them safely, take support of an expert or a trusted person. Dedicate half week to face each fear, soon they would lose their strength.

CHAPTER THREE

WEEK THREE - Your love?

Human life has become too mechanical, daily demands and routine of the life surpasses everything, even our hobbies and likings. People consistently discuss, at length, about overpowering routine, life hassles and stress. In this fight for survival they miss out on things they love most. These things are very close to their heart, which rejuvenates them, filling them with joy. But, most miss out to them. You will know about it if you could interact with your heart, instead of your mind. Mind tells you what is logical, while heart is the voice of your soul. This voice is pure enough to protect us from something which everyone is copying or is a fad. Your involvement in your hobbies recharges you and makes you more creative and productive. It makes you happier in life and improves your relations with others.

The daily requirements of life keeps you away from all this great stuff, it just keep getting postponed. You should regularly take reasonable breaks from work to regenerate yourself by involving in activities of your interest. Some like to be on a beach, some want to go on a long drive, some want to be with nature while others would go on an adventure. Do not postpone it more, do it now.

Action Step

You know what you love. This week try to take a required break from your daily life and immerse into your hobby.

CHAPTER FOUR

WEEK FOUR - Set deadlines

This week we will focus on becoming more effective. Productivity is the driving force to differentiate between success and failure. A more productive nation has stronger economy than others. A more productive company would become the best company in its industry. A more productive person would be appreciated and liked by an organization and would be eligible for more raises. If productivity is such a strong force then it should compel every person to become more productive. Everyone wants to improve their output but they may not know the easiest way to do it.

Work is like fluid which fills the allotted time. A work of one hour can fill five hours easily, if five hours are allotted to it. The same work can be completed in 45 minutes if a deadline is set to it, though it would require special skills and extensive efforts to do it. Definitely, the 45 minutes person would be more productive than one hour person and much more productive than 5 hours person. We will try to be as productive as the 45 minutes person. This accomplishment would require you to be more skillful and competent, but the right attitude carries maximum importance. It will also require a lot of efforts from your side, which may exhaust you, but it is worth the effort to aim at success. For the more 'productive you' the life would change radically which will be clearly observable from the interactions of your coworkers and partners.

For every task you need to decide on a reasonable but tight deadline, to which you would stick. It is important to notice that the required quality of the work is maintained in every possible way. You would meet this deadline with excellent results. Next time, you would improvise and find new ways to beat your previous deadline. You are more productive.

Action Step

This week identify one task, every-day, and try to be more productive in it. Write the chosen task of the day and the normal time it takes to complete it, also specify the new deadline. Write your plan or ideas to meet it. After meeting the deadline, write ways to improvise the process.

CHAPTER FIVE

WEEK FIVE – Find the right balance

The conflict between personal and professional life is everywhere. It seems that if you focus more on your professional life your personal life suffers and vice versa. Actually it is not so, both can be balanced and enjoyed completely. It is to be noted that both side feeds each other, a happy personal life makes your professional side better and the problems of professional side can spill over to your personal side, affecting it in wrong ways. As both combined make our life, we need success in both to live a fulfilled and happy life. Balancing both do not mean working from home, which is a choice many people make to save their commute time or to meet pressing needs at home. Some people sacrifice one for the other hoping to find completeness in life dedicating themselves in either personal or professional part. People make choices depending upon their own circumstances and life they want to live.

Balancing both sides of life would be a better option. It is good for families and it is good for the economy. But, keeping it balanced has always been considered complex. The problem arise when we act based on the instincts and lose our control on us to external forces, which put us into unwanted situations and stress. The demands of one side may force us to neglect the other side, thereby creating unnecessary tension.

We need to define our priorities in life, which would keep us happy and satisfied. This would allow us to design the right model for our personal and professional life. We just need to follow it with strict discipline.

Action Step

Do you find your personal and professional life unbalanced? If yes, you need to find the point of pressure, also what, where and why the balance is disturbed. You need to define your priorities in life and things which are important to you. Design a balanced plan for a better personal and professional life. Follow the finalized modal for this week.

CHAPTER SIX

WEEK SIX - Forgive

In our life we keep meeting lot of people, most of them are neutral for us, we have no emotional connect with them. We like many people, we love few and we hate some. We meet them in our offices, meetings, neighborhood, community, society and market. Some of them can be our colleagues and some can be our relatives & friends. We may hate them for insulting us, for their attitude, for their behavior or for the way they look & talk or for their actions. We do not like their presence as they make us uneasy. They seem to emit negativity which affects us in harmful ways. More we encounter them, more we tend to hate them. We cannot forgive them for what they are or the way they look. Here we are not including people with the tag 'dislike', whom we do not like. We used to like them but for some reasons we started disliking them; the reasons could be trivial for this feeling. We do not hate them and they could easily be forgiven.

The problem is that the feeling of hate is damaging for us too. It builds negativity in us. It is so strong that it overpowers our good feelings too. It leads us to lose our self-control and surrender this control to the external forces like 'the presence of hateful person'. This negative feeling impacts our body, mind and soul, which affects our present and future. It is losing too much for the person we hate. Sometimes, we engross ourselves in finding ways to make her feel bad, which is actually giving her more control of our feelings. The best revenge would be indifference.

We would focus on this aspect this week. If we could forgive the person we hate and become neutral to her, then it would save us from lot of pain. As our hate is not affecting anyone, except us, that too in harmful way, it is better to let it go. The moment you forgive, you would feel more relaxed and at ease with yourself. The stress level would go down and your happiness level would rise.

Action Step

Identify two people you hate and write their names. Think about the hateful feelings that has affected you in wrong ways and which would keep affecting you in future. Think about the sin of giving control of your feelings to external forces and person getting affected by this feeling is only you. Just forgive them for what they have done or what they are. You need not connect to them, but now you are neutral to them. Tear the page where you have written the names and throw it away. You are happier, more in control and with reduced stress.

CHAPTER SEVEN

WEEK SEVEN –
Connect

Life is a journey and in this journey we get connected with lot of people, we like some people we love some, we hate some. Few of these are those who get very close to us, who are lot like us. We like them for their genuineness, for their behavior, for their care and for their feelings towards us. We feel better with them and we have fun with them, they enrich our lives. There is some sort of connection which we do not feel with others. We share our secrets with them and they entrust us with their secrets. We discuss our problems and search for solutions. We motivate each other during the time of loss and provide support in pain. They looked like the extension to us and we felt incomplete without them. They were our 'best friends'. They are difficult to forget and remain with us for our whole life, in memories.

A friend is different in the sense that the emotional connect is not as strong as for the 'best friend'. You can enjoy with friends but you may not trust them completely. You would not share you pain and fears with them and you can forget them easily after you separate from them. It is much easier to find fiends than 'best friends'.

It has been many years now, even decades, we have not interacted with them. We are busy with our lives, hopefully they are with theirs. Most of the time the total number of these types of friends would be in single digits. We are sure that they are not the same as they were and must be lot different now. That connect with them which used to be at its peak is no more visible. We do not have their contact details and we do not feel the urge to make efforts to get that. It was our past, a nice past, we think. Even if we feel the urge to connect with them, they may not appreciate that, which would be embarrassing. Maybe, they also feel the same way.

This week we would connect with two of our past 'best friends', who are long lost in the speed of life. We would keep all hitch and hesitation aside and would make every effort to find their contact details. We will contact them and talk to them. Rest is up to you to experience.

Action Step

Identify two of your 'best friends', whose contact details can be obtained easily and get their telephone or mobile numbers. Find the best time to talk, call and talk to them.

CHAPTER EIGHT

WEEK EIGHT - Meditate

Life is too busy and we are always engaged in some or other things. Our mind is completely engaged with work and tasks to be completed. We have deadlines, we have releases, we have meetings and we have urgent items to complete. All this raises stress and tension in mind, which leads to diseases like heart attack, hypertension, diabetes etc. We all know this lifestyle is unsustainable and could harm us, but we feel helpless to do anything about it. This pressure makes us age faster and burn us out. This increases frustration and conflicts in our life. People feel less happy and more confused. Their productivity decreases and they feel dissatisfied at work.

People try to find solutions in either intoxication or anger or with spiritual gurus. First two are should be avoided while the third one preach a simple message. These gurus spread a simple message of meditation, as it is the source of everything. According to them through meditation you connect with universe which leads to peace and happiness. I will not comment on the whole concept as it is deep and debatable, but, meditation has many benefits. Meditation is the process of bringing mind at zero state, consciously, without thinking or imagining anything. Mind at this state is at peace and is completely calm, away from the problems of life. It would put mind to deep rest, which is working 24x7. People discover miraculous benefits of meditation, they get more energetic, positive, focused and more productive. They get clarity in decisions and creativity in solutions. Several ancient philosophies and thinking supports meditation, maybe presented in diverse forms. People also do it in different ways e.g. for starters, they close eyes and either imagine something beautiful & peaceful to focus or they recite a mantra for focusing all of their attention on it. The main idea is to forget about everything, past, present and future, during the time of meditation. Meditation is not about closing the eyes and thinking something or going to sleep. It is also not about dreaming in sleep or visualizing vague images. It is also not about getting absorbed in some performance or relaxing physically. It is disconnecting from the world for some time. Advanced practitioners can get into the meditative state in an instant and has ability to even meditate with open eyes. You can explore more for the process and methodology of meditation.

This week you should practice and experience meditation for some time every day. You can start with 5 minutes for day 1, 6 minutes for day 2, till 10 minutes for day 6, increasing one minute every day. You can do it anytime, but you should not be disturbed during the process. Your objective is to sit in a comfortable position, close your eyes and let your mind disconnect from the world. You can do this by revisiting a beautiful place in your mind, focusing on nature and observing the fine details of it like the shades of light yellow color on the leaves with drops of mist dancing on them. You can also focus on the light humming voice produced by you.

Action Step

Decide the time and location for practicing meditation. Find a place where you will not be disturbed for the required time. You need to sit in easy posture with back straight, close your eyes and meditate for five minutes for day 1, six minutes for day 2, seven minutes for day 3, eight minutes for day 4, nine minutes for day 5 and ten minutes for day 6.

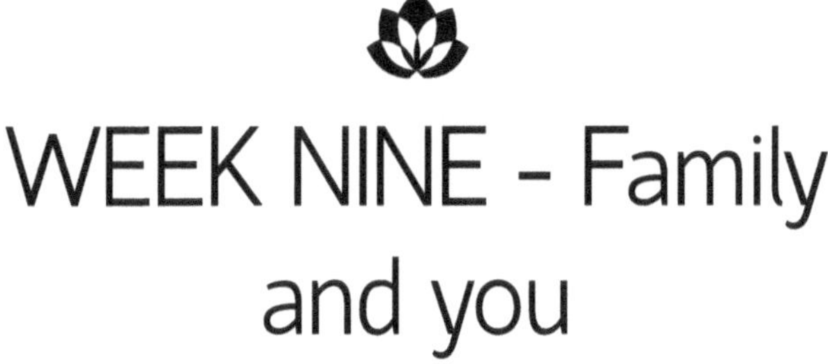

WEEK NINE – Family and you

Many important things which we possess are taken for granted, without realizing their value. This is a normal human nature; the preciousness of something gets visibility only after losing it. Life is awfully busy and for us the most precious resource is time, which is used to complete one task after another. Every day consists of scheduling and completing personal and professional tasks, which keep our emotions and mind completely occupied. Many people feel pathetic about the stuff they do not have, the latest luxury modal of car, the latest gadget, the smarter companion, the better job or something else. This desire is unending as meeting one raises another, then another, it goes on. We put our maximum efforts to meet them and put our life and soul to it. During this time we tend to miss out on the most precious people in our life, our family. We all love our families, but we take them for granted. Our family may consist of siblings, parents, wife, husband, kids or other close people like cousins and relatives. For them your happiness is of paramount importance. They know that you are busy and putting every effort to support the family. But they wish to get more of your time and love.

They want to spend more time with you, talk to you, play with you, shop with you, travel with you or just sit near you. But they never complain as they know your sincerity and responsibility. You are with them on weekends and holidays, you are with them on emergencies and crises, but that is either the part of routine or in exceptional circumstances. As we know that life is also about gathering as much happiness as possible, occasionally we can delight them with our time.

Sometimes, we can surprise them with the gift of our time, by taking them to a long pending fun trip or taking kids to a nearby park for playing with them or going on a movie together. This slight break of routine would have negligible costs but huge gains, these gains would be evident in the eyes of your family members who would be waiting for more surprises from you.

This week we would try to spend more time with our families, this does not mean taking a leave from work but to find ways break the strict routine to be with your family members, filling them with happiness. You can find creative ways to do that.

Action Step

Find ways to squeeze more time from your daily routine to be with your family. You know about what each member likes most; plan and do it for them, delighting each of them. Be innovative to do this on regular basis.

CHAPTER TEN

WEEK TEN - Stretch yourself

Though living every-day is full of risks, we tend to dislike it. There is some amount of risk while traveling, while arguing with boss, while shifting jobs or even in daily exercise routine. Taking this risk is so well embedded in our system that it is the part of life and our routine. Most of the time these risks do not affect us and are considered insignificant as their probability of happening is much less and these risks are faced by everyone, every-day. These risks also get reduced with familiarity and experience. In fact, they are not even considered as risks. Then there are some activities, which are not considered as risky, as element of risk is much less in those, but they make us uncomfortable, like flying in an airplane is almost risk free but it makes many people uncomfortable. Many people find adventure sports as challenging, some find taking some initiation in office as tough and few people will have fear of deep water.

In our work life most of us are restricted to the tasks assigned by the organization, without taking any challenges or initiations. Taking any challenge is considered risky as any wrong step may disturb the present perception about our abilities, even knowing that success would raise us further in our career. We are hesitant to even prepare for it by building skills and competencies. This hesitation comes either from our satisfaction with status-quo or lack of confidence or to avoid tough competition. This attitude keeps pushing us down in life and restricts us to realize our true earning potential. It is also affects our self-respect and self-esteem. Without realizing these costs we keep ourselves restricted to these imaginary boundaries, which works as lose-lose for us and for organization.

If we could get into the habit of taking challenges, which would be supported by right preparations from our side, then it would add significant value to our professional life. This would improve our prospects for career growth and improved earnings. It would make us more confident with stronger self-belief. Entrepreneurship is all about taking challenges with creativity and self-belief. We all should try to act like dynamic entrepreneurs within our organizations. This would create a winning environment for both us and organization, which can grow together.

This week we would prepare and then take some challenging tasks at work. We would try our best to complete those successfully, in time. To achieve this, we would take help from every resource and support available, but the task ownership lies with us i.e. we are completely responsible for the success and failure of the task. It does not mean that we vaguely take any assignment without any plan or logical thinking. The purpose of the challenging task is to stretch us a bit, it should make us take initiates and use all of our skills. It should also make us learn new skills, develop new competencies and force us to take tough decisions. Our work space would be full of these types of challenges, we need to choose our challenge or take an initiative.

Action Step

You know about your skills set and competencies. Identify a challenge at the workplace which suits your strengths, it should also push you a little forward. You can also look for some initiatives for meeting organizational goals. You need to take the complete ownership of the task, while you can take any help to complete the task satisfactorily.

CHAPTER ELEVEN

WEEK ELEVEN – What is you purpose?

If someone asks us about our objective of life the answer looks simple. First, we are alive so we have to live, we have responsibilities towards ourselves, our families and other people who are dependent on us, we want happiness, health, wealth, security; we want love, good food, luxury and peace of mind. More or less the objectives remain almost the same for most of us. If we look at other living beings like animals their objective in life is looking for food, security, reproduction, caring for young, finding a proper place to stay and just struggle live. We are very different from animals as we are gifted with intelligence and right body.

Every human being is much more capable than their daily performances in market and society. We have huge unused capacity of mind and body, ready to be tapped. This can be achieved through will-power, which is considered as the source of all our complex actions. Our lifestyle is guided by the economic and social conditions. We have tight schedules and busy lives, we have stacks of deadlines and urgent tasks. There is no wonder that the objective of life remains as defined above. Some can compare their life with a strong current of water, in which they find themselves floating. A working woman has to look after her office deadlines and also has responsibilities of her home and kids. A home-maker is completely busy with managing her family and home. Teenagers are busy with studies, digital and physical life's pressures. Elders, after toiling for their whole working life, enjoy their retirement with family and deal with the stresses of old age. If we look around, everyone, including us is busy with similar activities. If we ask someone about their purpose of life, either they do not understand it or consider it as short term objectives, which would include things like money, job, savings, relationship, security, health etc. For bringing clarity to this concept we need to understand that these basic things are not the purpose of life. These maybe necessities, needs or desires of life but not purpose. Almost all of these are pointed towards self to drive-out some benefit from each, which may take us away from pain and towards pleasure. As this is generally the way masses (people) think and feel, we tend to remain at the similar level of masses not to rise above it.

Purpose is different and much bigger than us. We must have observed some extraordinary individuals who seem to have infinite energy and clarity. They have strong sense of self-belief, self-respect, commitment and dedication. They have attractive personalities, high confidence and take firm decisions. Their strength seems to come from inside and their passion is very infectious, which seems to motivate everyone near them. This is something which animals cannot replicate. Even for most humans this is above their capacities, as they are not clear about the mystery attached to the power of purpose.

Achievers are driven by some purpose. It is a vision, which is not just self-oriented but much bigger than us. As this is big and may touch many others in positive way, it no longer remains restricted to us. Many people join it and support the cause honestly. As you are true to it, it gives you clarity in life to take decisions, it gives you self-belief to face any adversity, it provides you with energy abundance, it makes you better. This purpose can be related to your nation, humanity, society, community or your organization. You can be an entrepreneur and your purpose is to create the biggest company in your industry supporting thousands of jobs, providing excellent product & service to your customers and launching innovative solutions in the marketplace. You can have a political party focusing on eradicating the corruption and crime from your country, you can support an NGO educating poor kids and nurturing their future.

Purpose has amazing force in it, but you need to be honest towards it and true to yourself. This week we would find a strong purpose for our lives. You need to find something which is close to your heart and find the ways to contribute towards the goal. It should suit your skill set and daily schedule, as anything out of sync would have short life-span. Start with small steps towards it, with time you would find yourself more and more involved in it.

Action Steps

Write down all things for which you feel strongly and are close to your heart, which could be the pain you feel for hungry and homeless elders or you feel frustrated with the inefficiencies in your social system or something else. Find the ways to contribute to it without disturbing your daily life. Take one small action towards it.

CHAPTER TWELVE

WEEK TWELVE – Limiting beliefs

We are the sum of our beliefs. Our beliefs guide us to develop ideas and take action. Beliefs are responsible for our behavior and emotions. They control our mind and influence our decisions. The passions and limitations are decided by our beliefs. They make us strong or weak. They sit deep into our subconscious mind and are built over time through repeated experiences in life. Many start to take form while we were kids and become stronger as we age. By the time we are adults they become extremely strong and become the main decision maker in our lives, which can be good or bad based upon the choices we make.

Empowering beliefs give us strength and motivate us to take risks and persevere till we get success. They help us to feel hopeful and optimistic during hardships. They make us take tough decisions and give us strength. A deep faith in God is a belief, which gives us hope and positivity. This belief provides us with infinite source of energy to move forward and gives us confidence to aim for challenging tasks. If we get success the credit goes to the belief. Even during failures the belief is not shaken, instead we find logical answers to convince ourselves that God must have other plans for us, therefore, we are being instructed to change course. Such is the power of belief.

Belief should not be confused with temporary acceptance of some facts. If we accept a fact that a particular player is great, that is the acceptance of a fact but not belief, similarly, the liking for a newspaper doesn't mean we believe every word printed in it or views expressed by it.

Similar to empowering beliefs we have limiting beliefs, which acts like a stumbling block for everything we do. They will stop us from taking right decisions, they will block us from getting into a relationship or rebuilding a relationship and they will create resistance in improving ourselves and would create hindrances for our forward movement. We know about them but we are unable to break them, our inadequate efforts being the main culprit. A bad experience of a small girl with a man in childhood may build a belief to term all men bad, which will not let her get into healthy relationship with any man. A failure in an examination may build a belief system of fear for any test or assessment, which would shake her confidence, thereby strengthening this limiting belief. We do not seem to understand the damage they have done in our lives, as we are too busy living with them. They must be identified, weakened and removed from our system.

This week we will identify and eradicate some of our limiting beliefs. Identifying them would be the easiest part as we live with them and know their limitations. We need to identify them and write them clearly, we need to find the barriers they had always put for us to block our growth, happiness and success. To weaken them we should raise questions against it proving it illogical and foolish, supporting it by real life cases. You need to commit to turn against it and actually take required action to weaken it. This must be at the top of your mind for few days. The belief would lose strength. You need to take one limiting belief at a time.

Action Step

Identify two limiting beliefs stationed in your subconscious mind. You need to take one at a time and attack it with full force, in the way as specified before, for next three days. After weakening it, you can move onto next.

CHAPTER THIRTEEN

WEEK THIRTEEN – Power of action

We are different from animals mainly because of our mind, it makes us think better. Our intelligence and knowledge differentiate us from other humans. A smarter person would have great ideas and can create better plans and strategy. Better understanding would give us tools to grasp the market requirements in a better way to develop successful offerings. Superior ideas can equip us to create better products, services or companies.

Ideas would just remain ideas if they are not acted upon. They would be considered as cheap if not accompanied by action. Action is the main reason which differentiates a winner from a loser. Many people develop great plans but depend on others for action and implementers get the maximum appreciation. People are hesitant to action, either they lack confidence or are risk averse or don't trust their plans. This hesitation makes them weak at taking initiatives or accepting any responsibility. This attitude is detrimental for success and growth. People may know about this weakness but are not able to act against it. A person without action is actually choosing a life of mediocrity. Right action generally leads to desired results. A genuine action would be well thought, properly planned, completely equipped and correctly executed with excellence.

Action does not mean any vague act without thinking or planning. Cases are abound with people of action, who are bad at planning, competencies and execution, generally end up as failures. They are acting either based on instincts or half-backed information or wrong suggestions. They fail to use common sense or to analyze the action logically. Many move to action without putting genuine efforts to it, which may be directed to some cheap show-off or to satisfy their ego. These actions never work and are better to remain dormant, as they unnecessarily inflict cost and waste energy & time.

We may be an action person but we need to become more dynamic by making right choices. We should identify the reasons of hesitation for action and correct them.

Action Step

This week we would commit to action. If we are not an action person, we will become one; if we like and take actions then we would move towards greater dynamism. The focus is to push your boundaries further. We also need to analyze our output and check the quality of results, we may need to correct something by becoming better at execution.

CHAPTER FOURTEEN

WEEK FORTEEN - Right questions

We must have observed kids who have no hesitation and ask lot of questions. They learn through questions. Questions are like gift to humanity, the mind ask questions and then force us to search for answers. All humans also think through this process of asking questions. If we have to go from place A to place B, we take decision through a questioning process:

- Do I really have to go?
- What is my reason of going to B?
- Where are A and B located?
- What is the distance?
- What vehicles are available for travelling A to B?
- Which vehicle can take me fastest and cheapest?
- Do I want to go by this vehicle or I have other priorities?
- Should I leave now? If not, then when?

In fact all our daily thinking process can be broken down to similar set of questions. They also decide our depth of introspection and our width of reasoning. A shallow person may not ask many questions and would simply start to travel immediately with the vehicle she encounters first. A sharp person may ask many more questions to get more depth. In addition to asking questions, we also need the skills of answering them fast and in least possible time, as any delay would be compounded for delayed decisions. This understanding would help you to observe yourself and others in a better way.

Asking any illogical or unrelated question would not help to think better, instead it would only distract and confuse. We can see people blacking out sometimes, not able to comprehend anything, which could be a confused state of mind not able to manage the questioning and answering process properly.

As these questions carries big responsibility for quality of our thinking, they empower us too. If we could manage the process of asking empowering questions then our thinking would become better, more positive and with better perspectives. In any situation we may ask empowering questions to put our focus on right perspectives. A bad phase can be thought through with these questions:

- What are the reasons for this to happen?
- How can I work on these reasons?
- Why is it required to start a winning struggle with these reasons?
- What support I would need for it?
- Who can give me that support and how and when I should approach her?
- What can I learn from it so that it never happens again?
- Can I make it an opportunity for me?

This thinking process would lead your focus towards right direction and you would come out of the situation stronger.

A wrong thinking process may discourage you to take the right decisions and actions. It may weaken you during the time of crises or even depress you. A wrong thinking process would be guided by wrong set of questions, which would be asked by pessimists. This question set could look like:

- Why it happens to me always?
- Is it luck or I am cursed?
- If I could not come out of it then I am destroyed?
- If I am destroyed how would I meet my monthly costs?
- I am a failure and I cannot even live a normal life?
- I am feeling so bad that it is affecting my body, will I get any disease?

The answers to these questions would lead to more passive questions and this process is unending, unless it is broken by an external factor. A positive person, who would bring an empowering perception, could add great value in these situations.

Our task is to become a more positive person who would see any situation in positive light. You would control your thinking process in better ways and would create the right perception for every event in your life. You may create a set of empowering questions which should become the part of your life and they would guide your thinking process.

Action Step

We would commit to the positive outlook in life. We would also prepare a set of positive questions which would become the part of our system and help us in building empowering thinking.

CHAPTER FIFTEEN

WEEK FIFTEEN – Genuine you

Most of the time we know the right principles for living a successful life, sometimes we even try to follow some of these principles but lack consistency to follow through. We meet many people every day, but sometimes we come in contact with certain individuals who build instant rapport with us. We tend to like them and more we know about them the better they looks. These people may not the best looking or well-dressed but has some unique attraction. We feel easy and safe with them and have confidence to share our secrets, even in initial interactions. These are the people who can be trusted and we believe that they will not break our trust. Building trust is one the most important attribute in a relationship, trust is like adhesive in a relationship. Without it there is no relationship but a weak connection.

If trust is such a complex force then how some people are able to build it easily and so well? The answer may be hidden in their personalities and the way they act. Ask anyone about the person they trust and they would immediately talk about honesty, clarity and genuineness. A person leaving such impression has to be honest, which would be evident through her communication and actions. This impression builds better relationships and is good for business and social life. People try to build a good rapport by acting genuine but they need to understand that this cannot be performed, either you are genuine or not.

To get the advantages of good rapport with others you need to be authentic and genuine and people will come to you. You need to be true to yourself, you need to be honest with others, you need to respect your words and you need to have empathy with others. You can be straight forward and you need to be clear. A genuine person is harmless and he can be entrusted with secrets. This connection builds an emotional bond which leads to better relationships. This network of relationships would nurture your support system and make you a successful person.

We would try to explore the power of this concept. This can work only with new people as existing acquaintances had already made a rigid impression about us, which would take substantial time and efforts to recreate your new image. With new people rapport building would be much easier and effective. You need to first visualize the person who would create a similar connection with you, which would help you to have a fair understanding about the impact it creates. You also need to identify the changes & improvements required in you for being a genuine person. This could be about keeping your words (your actions meet your words), you speak truth and you do not break trust. You also need to have certain good qualities like punctuality, empathy, respecting others & self and having clarity of purpose. You also need to care, be firm and clear in communication and have right body language. This would be a start of a winning career.

Action Step

You would try to be a perfect genuine person for next several days and this effort is not limited to specific place, time or with specific person, rather it would be 24x7 effort. You need not focus on immediate results but you would be true to self and to people you interact. This discipline would help you to experience better reactions from others, which would empower you and build your strength.

WEEK SIXTEEN – Just laugh

Some people are more attractive than others, we want to be with them, interact and have fun. We would like to do business with them and see them prosper. They may not be rich, good looking or popular but add extensive value with their presence. Their entry would make everyone light-up in room and even stressed out people feel at ease. They consistently deliver maximum sales numbers and are among the best in supply management. Customers want to talk to them and take extra efforts to add value by giving suggestions for improving products and services. In organizations, their value proposition is more that the responsibilities assigned to them. People want to include them in their teams and organizations want to associate with them. They seem to love life and looks content & happy with everything.

These people are positive people. They smile a lot and laugh a lot, displaying their shining white teeth most of the time. They seem to enjoy what they do and seem to feel happy to meet someone. People with strong faith are generally free of fears and have belief on some higher powers to support them in their life. You would find them satisfied and content with life and they look relatively happier than others. They don't look fake and their smiles and happiness is genuine, which comes from their heart and is not only on the lips. It is also very contagious and gets transferred to anyone who comes in contact. The hate, anger, jealousy and pain reduce with their influence and no one seems to dislike them. They are popular and are known with their smiling attribute. They may not be great at work but their value addition is much higher than others.

Many people try to copy, temporarily, to be like these people and force themself to smile and laugh, which either looks fake or funny. People distrust them and want to keep distance from them. They know instinctively that the displayed happiness is false. This is also not about laughing loud trying to attract attention of others, which is considered rude and disturbing. These actors need to understand that by doing this they are damaging value not adding it.

Many people cannot smile or laugh, even if they try hard, so they should not try it till it comes to them naturally. If you are happy and satisfied with life and enjoy every moment of it then that happiness would be evident on your face, body and actions. You would smile and laugh more, which would be completely honest and genuine. We need not try very hard to look happy, it comes automatically.

Action Step

This week we would work towards knowing and feeling all good things in our life so that we know we deserve to be very happy to enjoy the moments of life. Our pains would seem to lose strength and they would change form to look more positive. We would also try to smile and laugh more than we usually do. We will feel the magic.

CHAPTER SEVENTEEN

WEEK SEVENTEEN - Learn something new

Human beings are gifted with many abilities which other living beings lack and among these abilities learning comes on the top. This is the ability which differentiates one human from others through her achievements leading to success and prosperity in life. We as kids are great learners; our intelligence is developed only due to inquiring, asking questions, finding solutions and learning. We all must have noticed the amazing growth of kids. Today's markets & economy also reward and appreciate the learners who keep updating themselves with latest knowledge and skills. A learner is that confident individual who can take big risks as she knows that her learning abilities would empower her to face obstacles and she would even learn from her failures. Whatever happens she would come out stronger to embrace next set of challenges for winning. An entrepreneur learns about the latent needs of the market to create a successful solution with her knowledge for the target segment. A marketing executive can learn about the dynamics of the market to manage company's products better. A sales person would be better at connecting with customers by learning the needs and demands of the buyer.

A couple which have patience to learn more about each other would build stronger relationships. A manager can learn about group psychology to manage the team better.

Most of us move away from this much needed learning process as we grow. For winners the learning abilities act as the competitive advantage in the market. Companies spend millions of dollars on big data to get more insights about their customers to capture bigger market share by serving them better. Learning cannot be done half-heartedly as those ill-conceived insights would have negative effects, which could lead us to commit huge sum of money to it, without any true value proposition. Similarly, any lack of efforts in learning about a person can spoil our relationship with that individual.

We need to get into the mode of continuous leaning. This learning can be a new skill or new subject or a foreign market or a new sport. Anything would work if the leaning is leading to positive effects in life. This learning would help us to think creatively from different perspectives and find new processes for better execution.

Action Step

Decide on one new skill to learn this week. It should be in sync with your interests and could provide immediate utility in work and life. Find best possible ways to get trained, suiting your daily routine. Learn it and use it.

CHAPTER EIGHTEEN

WEEK EIGHTEEN – Bring clarity in life

Many political scientists specify that masses, which include most of humanity, are a bunch of confused individuals. A strong leader has the ability to sway the masses towards an ideology, which can even be designed against them. Confusion is one of the biggest weaknesses of humans which lead to their exploitation and harassment. Confusion leads to wrong perceptions and bad decisions. Many times the knowledge possessed by many professionals is thorough enough to let them perform their tasks proficiently, but their interest lies somewhere else, which leads to problems in their career path. People not clear about themselves, their likes, dislikes, aims, strengths or weaknesses would push them to unsatisfactory life.

Clarity saves us from big costs and lots of pain. We need to have complete clarity in life, about ourselves, about our profession, about relationships and about our opinions. People without clear opinions are standing on shaky grounds, one strong argument pushes them to opponents' side, which makes them lose credibility & image. Most of us are aware about the solution to this problem but are too lazy to take any action.

Many people feel that they have clarity, in fact they do not. They get influenced by other's ideas and reasoning, their decisions are biased and they are clouded in their thoughts. They may show a brave face but are weak from inside. They always look for support and have low self-esteem. They get difficulty to earn respect and confidence of others.

A clear person knows the principles she stands for, things she would do and the things she will never do. They are clear and dynamic at taking decisions and do not look for support. They have strong sense to self-respect and do not confuse it with ego. They do not require approvals from others and view themselves with high esteem. People trust & like them and want to be with them.

Action Step

We know where we need more clarity in our life, both personal and professional. It would be great if you can write down all those areas which require some work for clarity. You need to do a session of self-analysis to know clearly about your principles, likes and dislikes. Take one point at a time, think deep and bring clarity in it by filling required data, information or insight. Finally take a decision on it.

WEEK NINETEEN –
Motivate one

My understanding of leadership put the skills of developing leaders at very high level. The best way to learn leadership is to create leaders; this process would build the leadership skills in you. Definitely, this effort must be in addition to other activities to be a true leader. Influence in the society is not proportional to money, contacts or competencies, which has their limitations. But if you could develop the skill of motivating people to do better in life then you can have limitless influence. This skill is not simple and easy to master which requires a lot of improvement from your side to be good at it. A person requiring motivation needs to respect and trust you. She should believe your morality and skills set. You also need to be an incredible trainer to lift her spirits to perform better.

Everyday managers grapple with this problem in their organizations. Most are looking for the magic solution to motivate their teams to improve productivity and effectiveness. They use 'carrot and stick' approach to synchronize their personal goals with organizational goals. Team members are used to these techniques and are immune to any effect these techniques could bring. They do not look at the manager as their role model and they are receiving instructions from her only because of her designation. It would be difficult for this manager to motivate her team.

Motivation can only flow on the bridges of mutual trust and respect. You need to become a person from whom people would like to get motivation. Steve Jobs was a great motivator and so is any President of United States of America. You need to earn that respect and trust that is possessed by few individuals. Your attitude, thinking, behavior, skills and actions would help you to achieve that level.

Action Step

Identify a person whom you feel requires motivation to achieve something in life. She is skillful but hasn't tasted success yet. You need to build a rapport with her and use all your skills to make her take tough but right actions and achieve success.

CHAPTER TWENTY

WEEK TWENTY –
Hard and smart

We are told that hard work differentiates a winner from a loser. But, we have seen many people who work very hard but earn a fraction of others earnings, we point to unskilled jobs for proving this point. There are different kinds of jobs, high paying skilled jobs and low paying unskilled jobs. Skilled jobs require certain skills to take a particular responsibility, accounting, legal, medical or banking all require a unique set of skills, while unskilled jobs can be done by any person who wants to do it. The requirement of an unskilled job is a repeated work performed by body in tough conditions. The differentiating factor is only hard work. For skilled work, a person has to work hard but in smart way to be more productive. For example, for doing a research work we should use Internet instead of physical resources at library as digital data is easier to search, find and browse. Instead of travelling for a meeting we could use video conferencing to save time, energy and cost.

We need to work work-hard, smartly. The resources of present time have made all of us much smarter than our previous generation. Smartness can be a differentiating factor but hard-work is a much bigger factor as people avoid working hard. Working hard without smartness or being too smart without right amount of work cannot make you successful, you need the right combination of both.

Commitment to a task makes a team to put their full energies to get results; they would use the right ingredients of hardness and smartness to perform excellently.

Action Step

Are you a hard worker or smart worker or somewhere in between? You need to analyze your previous performances at work to design the right combination of hard-work and smart-work. The easier way would be a blanket commitment to hard work while keeping an open mind with a focus on required results. You need to keep focus on the results and tune your actions for maximum productivity.

CHAPTER TWENTY-ONE

WEEK TWENTY ONE
- Effectiveness

The strength of country's economy depends upon the productivity of its workers, the average produced value of each worker in the country. More productivity would mean better income per person and stronger GDP. The difference between two executives at same level in a company would be clear from their productivity, the value added by each person to the organization. Person with more productivity is an asset to the company and has faster growth.

People are productive because of their skills, knowledge, management, capacity to work and motivation level. A passionate person would be much more productive than a person with lower interest in work. Similarly, your managerial skills to get work done would affect results. You need to work hard, you need to work smart and you need to work with enthusiasm. A productive person would get appreciation and rewards which would motivate her to put longer hours and be more innovative to perform even better. Companies use both techniques of reward and stick to motivate their employees to improve performance.

Productivity cannot be faked as it is clearly evident from results. A person completing a task with lesser time but poor results would not be called productive. Similarly, a high quality output with time overshoot isn't performing well. A person cannot talk her way to productivity, she need to prove herself by excelling other employees in performance.

We should live a productive and effective life; our work needs to be of high quality, efficient and with strong value proposition. This simple commitment would be a certain path to our dreams.

Action Step

We would analyze our daily output, the results we produce every day and their effectiveness. For starting we can start by asking the following question every morning:

"What value will I add today?"

And by the end of the day asking:

"What value have I added today?"

Try to be more productive and effective every-day to have a better answer by the end of the day.

CHAPTER TWENTY-TWO

WEEK TWENTY TWO
- Better me

Extraordinary individuals commit to the constant improvement in their lives. They strive every day to improve themselves. They commit to be 'a better person today than yesterday and a better person tomorrow than today'. This promise is the secret which differentiates between an ordinary and an extraordinary person. The day a person commits to it she puts herself on the path of a life of greatness. Speak with any successful person and you would find this belief at the center of her success story. These people endeavors to learn new things and become more productive to keep up with this principle. Initially the path looks extremely difficult but with time it becomes the habit, you keep growing without any conscious efforts.

Many people start with it but find it too difficult to follow; the main reason for failure is not practicality but the level of commitment. This is also a well-known management principle which is used by few successful Japanese companies to improve their processes continuously, thereby reducing cost and improving efficiency. Saints use this principle to deeper their connection with God.

A person planning to follow this principle would need to be extremely sincere about implementing it into her life; she needs to be completely committed to follow it every day without any break. She needs to ask herself every night about the improvement in her life and how she is better today than yesterday. Next day would be a new day to follow this principle.

Action Step

Prepare yourself to commit to the specified principle, please note that this should be a sincere commitment. Find out ways to follow it every day, finally test is before sleeping. You need to focus on small improvements only, not the big ones, as collectively they bring big change.

CHAPTER TWENTY-THREE

WEEK TWENTY THREE – Decisions

Humans are good at thinking, they can think vertically, laterally or radially. They have analytical and logical brain. They can be good at making plans and strategy. But, most are hesitant to take decisions as it involves taking responsibility. Person taking a decision is taking full responsibility of the consequences of that decision; she would be responsible for any success and all failures. Decision making is authoritative as the decision could be backed by huge resources and efforts. A decision to develop a product would require research and development, sourcing raw materials, manufacturing, marketing, selling and distribution. The future of the whole company could depend on this decision, with it the career of thousands of employees and promises to millions of customers. A special-forces commander has to take decisions which could jeopardize the mission and the lives of team-members.

Decision making requires experience, empathy, intuition, knowledge and responsibility. It cannot be taken lightly and should not be pushed to others. All organizations place extremely responsible and capable people at the decision making positions, hierarchy decides the level of decisions to be taken.

Similar challenges we face in our personal life where the responsibility of decision making lies entirely on us. Our decisions decide the life we live and shape the future. Many people regret their decisions and live a life in guilt. Many people keep postponing taking decisions because of the responsibility attached to it.

If we decide to be extremely serious about taking decisions and then take full responsibility for it then our life would be happier. We need to be fast in taking decisions and be flexible in making improvements in it. We must never regret our decisions as we take them best to our knowledge, intentions and with complete sincerity. These decisions are our own and we should never be apologetic for them, to anyone. You can learn from any fallout in past decisions for taking better decisions in future.

Action Step

Identify five decisions which are pending for quite some time. These decisions were not taken either due to lack of information, fear or laziness. These decisions could have impacted your life in some nice way. You need to take these decisions within this week.

CHAPTER TWENTY-FOUR

WEEK TWENTY FOUR - Read one good book

We learn from our experiences or from the experiences of others. Life is full of lessons about what works, what don't, what should be done, what shouldn't. Our interactions with others also guide us with insights from their life. A person living in big city can learn something from the life of a town dweller or from the experiences of a village person. An executive in manufacturing can learn about some best practices from IT industry or vice versa. A doctor can learn some unique skills from a lawyer and a lawyer can learn from an accountant.

Humanity has created the pool of vast knowledge which is growing at a rapid pace continuously. We can focus on a specific area or domain but we can always get a lot of new ideas from people exposed to other knowledge & experiences. A CEO of a company may not be an expert in one area but is supposed to have the required understanding of all divisions of the company, which is required to take intricate decisions. An open minded person who has better awareness than others would take better decisions and could have better probability of winning in life. We need to keep us exposed to new experiences and knowledge to perform better in life. Books are one way to do it.

Books are the essence of a topic which a writer wants to express in her writings. It could fiction or non-fiction, for our discussion we would focus on non-fiction. Books can be on new technologies listing new developments which can be used in our business, books can be on managing better or to lead effectively. Books can build a case for a specific political ideology and they can explain the problems in economy. They can be on self-help, skills development, current affairs or on new ideas for thinking effectively. We as intelligent humans know the power of books and the value they would add in our life. Sometimes, few gems are published which have enormous effect on the readers. We must have identified few; we even took the initiative of buying and displaying them in our library. But somehow, due to lack of time or some problems or laziness we were not able to read them. So much of knowledge is waiting to be grasped.

We would take them one by one and get the essence of each to use them for empowering ourselves.

Action step

Take one thin book, which you want to read for a long time and finish it this week.

WEEK TWENTY FIVE
– Why procrastinate?

We must have encountered some individuals, whose life seem to look perfect, all right things happen to them making them successful and happy. They live a simple life, they look like us, think life us and talk like us but they seem to get more rewards. We either consider it as luck or an unseen force helping them. We have tried to observe them closely to find the difference but it is not visible. The main difference is that they are action guys and never procrastinate anything. They are doers and also get things done.

Doers are intelligent people who are clear about the right action to be taken. They read, research, interact and decide on the right actions to be taken and without any delay they go ahead and act on it. They focus on results and keep iterating their actions till they get desired results.

Then there are people who are in the strict habit of procrastination. Anything which has to be done now can be done later and which has to be today can be done tomorrow, only problem being that 'later' and 'tomorrow' never comes. They are so much exposed to it that it has become their main habit, it guide their decisions. This habit has never been beneficial to them as they never gained anything out of it but they are its slave. People do not trust them and their promises are considered as vague talk. They do not build good relationships and are mostly considered as an irritant. Their life can change in an instant if they commit to break this negative habit now.

When we talk about action, we mean right action with required thinking put to it, not some ambiguous behavior which is termed as action.

We may also be in some influence of this habit of delaying actions. So many actions are waiting for the force of our energy. It is a natural reaction to postpone things but we need to fight that urge to 'do it now, just now'.

Action Step

This week, we would put ourselves out of the influence of procrastination and any of related behaviors. We would be doers and action persons who believe in taking immediate actions with focus on right results.

CHAPTER TWENTY-SIX

WEEK TWENTY SIX – Ethics and morality

If someone suggests us to act completely in moral and ethical ways, they may look out of touch with real world, as it is considered difficult for a moral person to live in this world. We believe that an ethical person cannot be successful or rich and it is considered that most of the rich are not completely moral and ethical.

Morality is more about doing the right things for the right reason as it benefits all, including us. If we act in a wrong way against a person we open a Pandora's Box as this behavior would compel her to act in immoral ways with other people. It becomes a chain reaction. Being moral also doesn't mean to act like a fool and people take advantage of you, it is assumed that you are a smart and intelligent person. In this context we would take morality as an action which would not harm, in any way, other human being. This is something which can easily be followed as this is right for the society and for us too. News channels are full of stories of people caught by law while acting in unethical and illegal ways.

Our actions are mostly legal, ethical and moral. Sometimes we act against it, maybe in minor way, with a small act, to have any noticeable harm on other person. It would be great if we could correct ourselves and be away from these minor actions also. It is said that every big criminal started with small crimes.

Action Step

We would commit not to act in any immoral, illegal or unethical way in our personal and professional life. If any occasion arises then we would simply choose to act against it or decently refuse the person requesting it.

WEEK TWENTY SEVEN - Contribute

Self-esteem is the value we feel about us while putting ourselves at that level. Do we need any approval or appreciation from others to feel good about ourselves or are we in control of our feelings? Many people have low self-esteem and they always need reassurances about themselves. They always have low confidence about their work or the way they look or the words they have spoken or the way they walk or anything else they do. Their confidence is controlled by others assurances and any wrong feedback put them in the state of panic. They are always tense and confused, as they are always concerned about the reaction of others.

Confident people have clarity in life and they get this feeling because of some skill, special attributes or past successes. They do not need approval of others, appreciations and criticisms carry similar weight. They do not care about the others views about them. They are informed, analytical and knowledgeable people and take firm decisions. These decisions are their own, not dictated or influenced by someone.

A successful person would be a confident person as repeated successes gives her confidence about her decisions. People with unique skill-set may also feel more confident and secure. These people have high self-esteem.

How can a normal person with low self-esteem build it, if you do not have big success or competencies? The simplest way to do is to contribute in some way. You can contribute to society, community or to your country. You need to do this without expecting any returns. This contribution should come from heart and it would give you a sense of satisfaction. If you are forcing yourself to contribute your time and efforts for any cause then it would lose its value. If you could contribute selflessly then your self-esteem would gain strength.

Action Step

You know your interests and hobbies. It would be great if you could link it to any type of contribution, without expecting anything in return.

CHAPTER TWENTY-EIGHT

WEEK TWENTY EIGHT - Exercise

Our body is like a place of worship and it should be treated as such. Our body and mind make us the individual people know about. A healthy body has a healthy mind and vice versa. We nurture our mind with knowledge, experiences, information, insights, creativity and deep thinking. A strong mind is the key to success and an associate of our emotions.

We are too busy with our personal and professional life and our time is completely engaged with solving day-to-day problems and completing urgent tasks. This makes us forget our responsibility towards our bodies. The pressure of time forces us to eat junk foods and drink fluids which could harm our bodies. Our office deadlines make us strain our bodies to its limits, and the speed of our daily life put our bodies consistently in pressure. Our bodies deserve more respect and care.

Every nation is grappling with the problem of obesity and deteriorating health, the reasons range from modern lifestyle to eating habits to lack of exercise. It is time that that we provide long due respect and love to our bodies.

We all know the benefits of physical exercises but we rarely get time to do it. Most people do not get the required time to exercise; we could be one of those. But, we also know the reality that it is not the deficiency of time but the lack of motivation to do it. This also makes us very creative in discovering strange reasons, to convince ourselves, about the difficulties of exercising. The only way is to decide and take strict conscious efforts to exercise daily.

Action Steps

We will dedicate this week to physical exercises. You can find some simple exercises, which suit your body, and exercise for next six days regularly. You need to be careful about not straining your body too much and you must immediately stop the schedule if you feel any discomfort. The schedule for next six days is as follows:

Day 1 – 5 minutes

Day 2 – 6 minutes

Day 3 – 7 minutes

Day 4 – 8 minutes

Day 5 – 9 minutes

Day 6 – 10 minutes

You can choose any time of the day, but you need to be careful about the regularity of the schedule. You need to do it, every-day, even if it is only for five minutes.

CHAPTER TWENTY-NINE

WEEK TWENTY NINE
- Be stylish

A person is known by her personality, knowledge and character. These three are the important pillars for every human being. People feel attracted to individuals with these characteristics and we tend to appreciate them. Leaders are supposed to have the right combination of personality, knowledge and character and we consider them as our role models.

Other celebrities like movie actors, singers and anchors are known by their acting, presentation, styles and controversies. Most of the time these people are always well dressed, groomed and in style. They wear latest fashion accessories, carry latest gadgets and walk with confidence. The whole media talk and write about them and people love them.

Humans feel appreciative for persons who take care of themselves, who are optimally dressed, well groomed and have style. We can notice them in markets, shopping malls, functions, offices and in society. We compliment them and want to be like them, people can hate them but they cannot be ignored. We can learn few things from them that we need to be well dressed and stylish always.

Action Step

Analyze yourself or take professional help to become a more stylish and groomed person. You can observe the difference in the attitude of people towards you.

CHAPTER THIRTY

WEEK THIRTY – Physiology and body language

Communication is one of the most important component of humanity. We communicate to express ourselves or to convince someone for our views. Our relationships become stronger through right communication and we convince the recruiter for job through impressive communication. Communication helps people to join their proficiencies to create a new product and a political leader inspires citizens to choose her for leading.

It is considered that a perfect communication is the combination of voice and body language. Body language is the expressive force of body working in synchronization with spoken words to communicate better. Words without body language would communicate only a part of the message to be delivered to the listener and that too will not have any impact. To be a perfect communicator we need to have a perfect body language.

A right body language also affects our emotions and moods. A dull posture would make us think negatively which in turn make us feel weak. While an energetic body would make us feel better and more positive. An active body would lead us to take actions.

We need to have the positive body posture and body language. Our talks should be supported with right and expressive body language.

Action Step

This week you need to have a right and active body posture with straight back and active body parts. Your verbal communication would be accompanied by an open and positive body language.

CHAPTER THIRTY-ONE

WEEK THIRTY ONE – Peak performance

The capacity of every human being is much more than actually used by each of them. We have seen extraordinary feats achieved by average looking people during the time of crises. Ordinary workers can take leadership positions to take responsibility to fight oppressive forces. The history books are full of similar examples of several others extraordinary human beings. The fact is that every human being can perform at same level if she decides to do so.

The mind and body have amazing capacities for extraordinary actions. But, most of the people are not able to experience it as they restrict themselves with limitations. They do not make the conscious efforts to reach this level of peak performance.

Peak performance is the level at which an individual uses all of her strengths to perform the task in hand. She would use her mental, emotional and physical resources to complete the work to its perfection. The mind is a perfect driving force to control our actions. We perform at our peak when we protect our families from crises or commit to a work with critical importance. This means that we can control our performance level which could be extremely high; generally the default level is set much lower.

Commitment provides the required energy to make us raise our level of performance. If we commit to something, our mind tags it as critical and then forces us to complete it in best possible way. An entrepreneur who has sacrificed everything to build an organization would work at her peak and take every possible action, however hard, to get success. A word of caution, this level of performance can be straining for body and mind, so we need to find a balanced approach to get our things done.

Action Step

You need to experience your peak performance. You can remember about any time in past you performed at you peak level or you can commit to a task, however small, and focus your energy towards it. You can use this ability to create wonders in your life.

CHAPTER THIRTY-TWO

WEEK THIRTY TWO – Trust breakers

Our daily life is full of interactions with various people. We always have a set of tasks, both personal and professional to be completed, and take every effort to complete them. Our focus is task, its completion and output. For its completion, sometimes we lie, break trust and make fool of people. These activities look normal and seem to not harm anyone. But over long time, these daily activities become our habit and affect our personality. We tend to develop some sort of fear, sitting deep inside, about people reacting to this behavior. People distrust us and we never get the benefit of doubt.

This type of personality does not earn respect of others and lose support during crises situations. They can never achieve leadership positions and struggle to build rapport with new acquaintances. We are acquainted with few people with similar personality and know our feelings for them. We should not be like them.

To start, we need to break the habit of casually speaking false, deceiving someone or breaking trust of people. With time we need to eradicate these habits completely from our psychology. The effect of these changes would not be evident immediately but overtime you would appreciate yourself for taking this decision.

Action Step

You need to decide and commit to above mentioned point and follow it in your life.

CHAPTER THIRTY-THREE

WEEK THIRTY THREE
- Dignity of others

"We need to behave the same way, we want to be treated". People at the position of power sometimes get in the mode of superiority complex and are extremely proud of their achievements. They rightly deserve that kind of feeling as they are winners and have achieved much more than others. These people are intelligent, hardworking and smart. They are doer and achievers who take initiatives and lead projects. They are assets to the organization and are treated as heroes. They are risk-takers who challenge the status quo and discover new solutions. They are responsible for the success of the organization and management takes all efforts not to let them leave the firm.

This special treatment to stars of the company sometimes makes few of them arrogant and rude. They mistreat their fellow employees and insult them. They attack the self-respect of low performing employees and hurt their dignity. They feel themselves as infallible and above the law of the company. This attitude of winners is despicable and shameful.

Every human deserve respect and love. She is born as human and has inalienable rights of freedom and respect and no-one can and should hurt her honor and dignity. We need to act in a way to resist this type of behavior.

Action Step

We would commit not to hurt the dignity and self-respect of any individual, however small or weak. We would also resist this behavior if we encounter any.

CHAPTER THIRTY-FOUR

WEEK THIRTY FOUR – The worst enemy

When a normal man behaves as abnormal? An angry person can be considered as mad as she is not in control of her senses and can harm anyone. We must have also observed this momentary insanity during our bursts of anger. Most of the crimes are committed in the fit of anger and hate. This feeling is extremely strong and looks difficult to control.

Losing self-control means losing control of external forces, which could be intelligent or eccentric. A person can be annoyed with the weather and deteriorating weather makes her angrier. Another can be irritated with the economic conditions of the economy and her job loss makes her loose mind with anger. They all know fully well that their actions would add no value in improving the situation, but they feel helpless. A person can be under severe stress and loses temper during a meeting with boss, which could be harmful for her career growth.

We as normal human beings have similar weaknesses; anger, hate and jealousy which make us lose our self-control and act wildly. It must be controlled for the benefit of all, including us. Meditation can of great help to improve our patience and control, so is reasoning. Asking the right question at right time can help to lessen the intensity of anger. The question could be "How will it help to solve the problem?" and "How is this behavior going to hurt me?" A dedicated conscious effort is required to eradicate these negative behaviors from your mental system.

Action Step

You need to do a self-analysis for your weaknesses, and think about the ways to weaken them. You can meditate and discover new ways to eliminate these dark behaviors from our system.

CHAPTER THIRTY-FIVE

WEEK THIRTY FIVE – Fear from whom?

Risk taking capabilities differentiates a person in confidence, skills & competencies, earning potential and optimism. Risk takers work at their peak performance and are learners. They are optimistic and have positive attitude in life. They look for opportunities and act on them. They know the ways to face their fears.

Fear is biggest resisting force for every human and each one has different type of fears. Fear makes us risk averse, which leads to a lack in initiation. Fear also affects our decision making capabilities which force us to make biased decisions. Fear affects our career prospects, relationships and life. It makes us weak and can even affects our daily life; witnessing a severe accident may create a phobia of travelling on roads, an experience of cash crunch can make us risk averse and a job loss can affect our performance in next one.

If somehow we could be detached from our fears then world opens for us with opportunities. Many pleasures of life, which were blocked from us, come to us and life looks better. Without fear we can perform better at job and can build healthier relationships, we can create companies and explore new places to have fun.

Fear can only be trounced by fighting it not by running from it. Fear loses its strength when faced with courage, as fear is only a perception of mind, not reality. When faced, the perception of the reality changes to positive and fear vanishes. A stage fear becomes extremely weak if attacked with performances on stage, a fear of driving an airplane goes with driving it and taking initiations would remove our fear of taking responsibilities.

We should face our fears. We can prepare ourselves for it, get required support, have courage and face it.

Action Step

Identity three of you fears, find effective but safe ways to face them, prepare for them and face each of them to give you freedom from certain restriction self-imposed by your mind.

CHAPTER THIRTY-SIX

WEEK THIRTY SIX – Good night sleep

We know hard work pays and most people work extremely hard to afford a nice life for themselves and for their families. They work for long hours straining their bodies to extreme limits. Some even sacrifice their holidays to meet deadlines and complete urgent tasks. The daily demands of life take a toll on our sleep.

Sleep is a process to give rest to rest our body and mind, which is important for healthy body and better thinking. It is considered that a person should sleep for about 7 hours a day to have freshness of body and mind. The lack of sleep can lead to low performance at work and lesser efficiency in other tasks. It may disturb the normal functioning of body and affect creativity. It may reduce the body's resistance capacities and make it more prone to diseases. The stress level increases, which could affect our daily life in negative ways.

We need to make sure that we complete our sleep daily, the benefits could be witnessed the next day. The sleep should be a sound sleep, without any disturbances or breaks. We need a comfortable place and right environment to get the true benefits of sleep.

Action Step

This week have a complete and gratifying sleep every day.

CHAPTER THIRTY-SEVEN

WEEK THIRTY SEVEN
– Goals

The magic formula in the science of achieving is to set goals, prepare, take action and achieve them, then again set new goals. Keep repeating this process until you achieve your dreams, and then move on to bigger dreams. Setting and accomplishing goals is the smallest unit for achievers and they perfect it over time.

Goal setting focuses our energies towards a specific direction helping us by providing clarity to take right decisions and actions. It would stretch us to perform at higher levels to get desired results. All companies follow this principle by giving certain sales and operations targets to be achieved by teams, which would support in meeting organizational revenue and profitability targets. Same principle can be used in personal life to accomplish personal targets, which could be daily, weekly or monthly.

If we could get into the habit of setting and achieving goals then our list of achievements would grow consistently. We need to show complete sincerity in this process as any dishonesty would lead to defeating the vary purpose of goal setting. We need to set stretched goals, which would make us work at higher level of efficiency to achieve the required results. The successful results would motivate us to move on to next set of goals.

Action Step

We need to set one personal and one professional stretched goal for the week. The expectation of results must be defined clearly. We should prepare our action plan to achieve these goals with a list of resources required to meet deadlines. We can also create our daily targets for these goals.

CHAPTER THIRTY-EIGHT

WEEK THIRTY EIGHT
- Elders

Our immediate family consists of our spouse, our kids and our elders. In eastern countries some people live in joint families including even some distant relatives, which have its pros and cons. But in most cities around the world increasing number of people live in nuclear families, which include their spouse and kids while elders stay separately in a different house.

Life is busy and people are busy in meeting its daily requirements. Weekdays are spent in work and weekends with immediate families and personal work. In this hustle, we tend to miss out on our elders and the time they deserve. They may love to spend time with us and their grandkids, which makes them happy, but have their limitations to travel. They are a part of our family and also deserve a part of our life and time.

Action Step

If you have elders in your family and somehow you have missed out to visit them for quite some time then now is the time. Plan to visit them this week and give then the happiness they deserve and are waiting to experience it for a long time.

CHAPTER THIRTY-NINE

WEEK THIRTY NINE – The source

We all have met achievers and leaders and they have excellent personalities, they are doers and seem to have extensive energy. They have unshakable belief on self and don't need approval from others to feel good about themselves. They are full of positivity and optimism and enjoy life to fullest.

This energy of leaders comes from inside and is never external, which means that her belief in self, faith in something and focus on a bigger purpose gives her the required motivation and dynamism to perform complex tasks. This makes her learn new things, take initiatives and risks to move towards her goals and vision.

Faith is the most powerful motivator for excelling in life. Faith is the belief and trust on something which is much bigger than us and solid as rock. Some people have faith on God or some higher powers, which gives them an attitude of a winner. This belief gives them a feeling that they would be guided and supported by their God and they are born to win, even a defeat is viewed from a positive perspective. This gives them optimism and hope about the present and future. With this winning belief they take huge challenges and meet extraordinary targets. This is the main secret of success.

Some people are atheist and they do not believe in God, but that place can be replaced by a guru, mentor or a guide. Some people believe on the existence of an intelligent energy, which controls everything while others have a superior confidence on self. Everything is fine if you have an infallible faith and belief which gives you required energy to win in life.

Action Step

You know about your faith. It could be your God, Guru, Mentor, Guide or Teacher. Whenever possible you should spend more time with that source of your power. The purpose is to strengthen your faith and divert that positivity for moving towards your purpose by achieving goals and winning in life.

CHAPTER FORTY

WEEK FORTY - Let it go

To desire is human. We desire many things in life but we are only able to achieve few. We also know that a fulfilled desire reduces its intensity and it cease to be a desire. A person desiring for a sports car removes it from the list of desire after she possesses one, the same goes for others. But, the ones we are not able to achieve keep the intensity of desire high. We all have several unfulfilled desires. Sometimes, they may have some harmful effect on us as its urge may force us to act immorally; a person can steal money to buy some object of desire, which is illegal and have its consequences. Sometimes, it can go up to the level of madness.

Luckily, we all have better self-control and we use it in positive ways. Some wishes are just unachievable and they keep troubling us for ages, even the whole life. People even die with grief and regrets for some unfulfilled wishes. We should let them go. These wishes which are not adding any value and affecting us negatively should be left for good. We need to just decide to do it.

Action Step

We all have some desires and unfulfilled wishes which are troubling us for a long time and have never added value to us through motivation or enthusiasm. We need to decide to remove them from the position of wish and desire. Identify two of these and let them go to never feel them again.

CHAPTER FORTY-ONE

WEEK FORTY ONE – Weaknesses – kill them

Every human has weaknesses and during self-analysis we generally find more weaknesses than strengths. We are aware about them and know their costs, but they are so much embedded in our system that it looks difficult to remove them. Weaknesses build over time during our upbringing, environment or our choice. We can be in the habit is procrastination, which was once our decision, now it is a habit. We can have stage fear, which could due to lack of opportunities during our school days. We may be risk-averse because we never took risk.

We know that if we work on our weaknesses for improvement, they would become our strengths, which would give us more happiness and prosperity. Even this understanding does not make us take steps to weaken our weaknesses. The reason could be the feeling about its overpowering rigidity or lack of time or lack of will.

A weakness would cease to exist if we decide to take some strict action against it. The two step process would be as follows:

- We know the cost of this weakness in our life and we decide to act against it.
- We take serious actions opposing it

For example, we know the price of procrastination in our life and we decide to eradicate it from our life. To follow on this decision, we would stop any type of procrastinating, however small, and become a person of action. We can enjoy the benefits of this new strength, thereby weakening the weakness. Consistency in this process would eliminate it from our life.

Action Step

Identify one of your weaknesses which you want to attack. You need to commit for the consistency of this attack, till it ceases to exist. By following the above mentioned technique you should initiate your attack against your weaknesses.

CHAPTER FORTY-TWO

WEEK FORTY TWO – Stronger you

The abilities in life can be broken down into a set of strengths, which make us unique and talented. More the number of strengths, more able we are and more we can achieve in life. These strengths are built in us during our upbringing, our experiences and our efforts. We could be a great sales person with our field experiences or we are good at managing perfect relationships with empathy or we are great communicator as we were trained for it since beginning.

These strengths make us perform superior at work and manage home effectively, they make us face challenges and take initiatives, and they make us hopeful & positive about our future. Many people consistently work towards increasing strengths in them; a technical person can learn management skills to manage a business unit or you can train yourself to take risks to start an IT company.

A person working on her strengths would be a more attractive and successful person than others. She would be a learner with strong will power to develop new skills and competencies. She cannot be hold down for long as next day she is equipped to fight. She can take responsibilities and can be trusted with execution. She focuses on results and has confidence to achieve them.

Developing strengths is one of the easiest process, if you commit to it. You need to choose a required strength which would add substantial value in your personal and professional life and find ways to develop it. And, you start developing it immediately, without any delays. You can put a deadline for its mastery and should be used repeatedly to make it implant in your system, firmly.

Action Step

Identify a strength to be developed, look for the resources required and take all possible steps to develop it. You need to practice it continuously till it naturally occurs to you.

CHAPTER FORTY-THREE

WEEK FORTY THREE
- Kids and gifts

We all love to receive gifts and surprises. It excites us and make us feel appreciated, loved and wanted. We must have observed this in our life that a person who surprises and gives us pleasure leaves a make in our life. This creates an emotional connection which lasts.

Children are emotional people rather than logical. You cannot win them with logic, you need to like and love them, truly, to get their attention. Children love gifts and it is the easiest way to get their attention and appreciation. You can observe the curiosity and happiness in the eyes of kids while receiving gifts. We can find interesting reasons to give them gifts.

Actions Steps

Identify five kids who know you, do some research about their like and dislikes and send them gifts. It would be great if you can personally deliver those, but for busy folks courier would be fine. You can be creative to find a unique reason for gifting.

CHAPTER FORTY-FOUR

WEEK FORTY FOUR - Nature

We are a part of nature and our body consists of the elements of nature. Nature is the provider of most of the resources to us, whether it is fresh air, water or food. We all like the freshness of the mornings and breeze of the evenings, we like mystery of mountains and calmness of oceans and we appreciate the greenness of forests and beauty of snow. Nature gives us peace and strengthens our creative muscles. Nature is our greatest teacher.

Modern day lifestyle consists of a busy life in a big city with 'to-do' lists and deficiency of time. We are not able to spend time with our loved ones and avoid caring for our bodies. This is responsible for stress and diseases. We lose our creativity and struggle to find happiness and connection. We accept this as our way of life and spend our life with it.

If we could connect with nature, on a regular basis, then our view of everything changes. We get more peace and control in life, we tend to forgive others and find happiness within ourselves, we would spread positivity and love simplicity. This connection with nature can be in any form, it could be a walk in jungle, mountain tracking, spending time at a beach or just having fun in a park. Peaceful morning and evening times are best suited for this type of connection.

Action Step

Find a suitable time and place to connect and experience nature, you can also choose different places for various days of the week. Your main purpose is to spend some time with nature, alone, feeling and appreciating it.

CHAPTER FORTY-FIVE

WEEK FORTY FIVE -
Hidden time

City life has its perils, pollution, noise, its pace, traffic and commuting. Many people live outside the cities but need to travel to work which consumes a lot of energy and time. You either commute by public transport options like buses & trains or you travel by your own vehicles like cars & two-wheelers. If you are driving then you need to put attention to driving and to protect yourself from rash drivers. If you use public transport to commute then it has its own challenges. This commute time can range from few minutes to more than an hour. If we add all then we waste quite some time in commuting, every-day.

If we could use this time more productively then it may have positive effects on our life. We can learn something, think about a solution, entertain ourselves with music or just talk to someone. Most people choose to entertain themselves, which is a nice way to commute. But sometimes, if we could use it to listen to an e-magazine or learn about a new management tool, it can be immediately put to use to add certain value to our work. The objective is to use our time more productively. We can find new ways to do it or we can use latest technology gadgets to support us in our learning process. Using this time more productively would shift us few hours ahead to ours peers, every week. This learning attitude can support our professional & personal growth.

Action Step

Identify the best ways to use your commute more productively. Get the required material and transform your commute to a learning session.

CHAPTER FORTY-SIX

WEEK FORTY SIX – Limitless

This week I want you to feel and experience limitlessness. This is a concept when you are free of any limiting thinking, beliefs or ideas by breaking all mental barriers, constraints and obstructions. You are free to do anything without any fear or concern of losing. You need to feel yourself all-powerful to achieve everything you want in your life. You are an action person who can take initiatives and challenges. You are not shy or have any hitch or mental blockage to achieve goals. You are clear about your purpose and vision and you are completely equipped to get it. This limitless feeling gives you clarity about your dreams. It describes the process to get it and the points of resistance. You feel motivated to move forward and feel the strength of achieving it. You will also observe the reasons of your fears and the ways to counter those, the mental barriers which have stopped you to work at your peak and motivations to take risks. You feel the power of creative force. You enjoy this process.

Action Step

Every-day you need to keep experiencing this to feel the positive energy inside you.

CHAPTER FORTY-SEVEN

WEEK FORTY SEVEN
- Gold and listening

We all have a certain view of the world and feel it the right way of describing it. With this view we label things as right or wrong, some people considers intoxication right while others may consider it wrong. We see the events of the world from this lens and find everything in same color. We have logical reasoning for it and have the energy to prove it right. Some people would put their energy and soul to prove the merits of superstitions and the future sufferings of people not following it. We are always ready to prove our point while neglecting others point of view. We need a lot of patience to hear points proposed by others, which we do not have. Most of the times we want to speak our mind and want others to listen. A person absorbed in a political ideology will have difficulty to listen to the merits of any other ideology.

We want to talk about our sufferings and problems, we want to talk about our achievements and we want to talk about the greatness of our future plans. We feel gratification by doing this and want to experience the response of others.

A person who only talks and never listens is the worst kind of communicator, she normally irritates her audience. This person is a bad learner and avoids reality. Her narrow view of the world is only possible description about the reality. People avoid them and consider them as frustrating; their knowledge is limited and creativity zero.

The best communicators are excellent listeners. They speak less and listen more, and when they speak they 'Speak Gold', with quality content, with optimized words which are delivered politely. Their few spoken words are more impactful than hundreds of others. They considers their words as precious, which are rightly so. They listen to others with impeccable sincerity, with eye contact and right body language. They seem to take interest in the talks of the speaker, who is immersed in sharing her emotions or views. The good communicators focus on creating impact instead to numbers of words spoken by them.

We should learn the art of listening.

Action Step

This week we would focus on our communication style and would try to become a better communicator. We first need to observe the patterns of our communication, and if done rightly, we can easily identify the problems in it. Our focus is to become a good listener who would genuinely listen to others and speak with optimum words to create the maximum impact in conversation.

CHAPTER FORTY-EIGHT

WEEK FORTY EIGHT – Open eyes dreams

We all have dreams, not which we see while sleeping but the ones we see with open eyes. This dream is our life's goal, something we want to achieve in this life. This could be the celebrity status, or a dream house or selling your products all over the world. Generally, dreams are big and looks difficult to achieve, therefore, most people considers it only a desire without any likelihood of its realization.

The achievers are different in the way that they consider it a goal instead of a desire. They plan and take decisions and actions towards achieving it. If the dream is too big, they break it up into parts and create milestones. They put their best and genuine efforts to achieve it, they may or may-not always achieve it, but they sincerely try for it.

People without a dream do not have big ambitions in life; they are satisfied with their existing achievements and just want to hold them. They want to graduate to the next level but with the speed as defined by the market not with any acceleration. They do not feel the need to work very hard or learn new things, unless forced onto them, as this attitude works for them. They are like most of the people around them and can easily hide amongst them. They don't affect the environment in anyway but the environment controls them, they flow with it and considers rightly placed in it. They 'go with the flow'.

We need to decide our place in above two categories; either we are a dreamer or want to go with flow. If we are a dreamer then we need to act on it, we need to plan and then take the first step.

Action Step

You need a complete clarity of your dream or ambition, then you must feel your right and responsibility to get it. You need to find ways to move towards it and finally take one action to set the ball rolling.

CHAPTER FORTY-NINE

WEEK FORTY NINE – Bad addictions

Addiction is our act of repeating something which has negative effect on us. We know about its ill-effects but we are unable to leave it for various reasons. We could be psychologically connected to it or our body and mind demands it. Person consuming drugs is addicted to it, she feel the intense need to consume it every day as without it she experiences unbearable pain. A person addicted to smoking needs to put extensive efforts to leave it.

Most of the addictions are not as intense as mentioned above, but they leave harmful effect on us. We could be addicted to fast foods and likes to consume them regularly, knowing its ill effects on our body. Some goes on shopping spree, knowing its effects on monthly budget. Some are addicted to watching television, knowing it kills precious time and its strain on eyes.

If we count our addictions, there could be many and they had impacted us in wrong way. For severe addictions like drug consumption we need medical treatment and guidance. For others, the will to leave is enough. You need to decide it, commit to it and never do it again. If you want to leave your addiction to fast foods, which you consume daily, you would need to decide to follow a strict discipline in it by consuming it once a fortnight instead of daily. If it is difficult you can take some expert advice.

Action Step

You need to leave one bad addition this week. Identify one, use your will power and discipline to leave it. You can also take some professional help, if required.

CHAPTER FIFTY

WEEK FIFTY – More opportunities

Perception is such a lens, which colors everything with the color of the lens. If the color is blue, everything would look blue; if it is red everything would be covered with red color. We also need to understand that the reality and facts remain the way they are, they never changes. We can look them from a negative perspective and find everything wrong with it or if we look the same facts from a different angle they would look full of opportunities. A sales person of shoes was sent to a village in a poor country for selling shoes, she called back immediately telling manager about the zero prospects of selling shoes as everyone lives barefoot. Another sales-person looks it as an opportunity as she can sell shoes to everyone. It just the way of looking at reality.

Positive people find opportunities everywhere while negative people do not see it anywhere. This is a clear difference between winners and losers.

We may have our way of looking at things; we also have several problems in our life. We do not score good marks in examination or we do not get the right job. We always mess up in our relationships or we are considered as a loser in life. Human life is full of problems or full of opportunities depends upon person to person. The problems of one person can be opportunities for other. We need to ask right questions to view the 'so-called' problems in a different light. We discussed about the power of asking right questions in Week Fourteen.

Action Step

Identify two of your problems, and check what questions you were asking till now. Prepare a different set of questions and convert these problems into new opportunities for you.

CHAPTER FIFTY-ONE

WEEK FIFTY ONE - Perception changes everything

There are no negatives and positives in life there are only events. These events can be tagged as negative or positive based on our perception of it. A person with all types of hardships in her life can become the owner of a successful company as for her every event took her towards her goals of owning a company, while another person with beautiful childhood can end up struggling as for her the life was full of thorns. Positive people are not blessed people who get everything right in their lives; instead they view everything as positive, full of opportunities. A negative person has everything wrong in her life as she views it that way. The difference is as simple as the way of looking at things and situations.

We all have several events in our life, it would be great if we can perceive them in positive light. This small difference can save us from pain and heartburns, instead it would give us new strength and positivity.

Action Step

Identify three past events in your life which you consider as negative and perceive them as positive. You can use questioning technique, as discussed before, to weaken the negative perception and creating a fresh and positive view of these events.

CHAPTER FIFTY-TWO

WEEK FIFTY TWO – The start of journey

Your journey of one year completes this week. During this time we explored and experienced several techniques to make our life better and successful. You may not carry all the leanings of this book but if it added some value in your life the process of transformation has already begun. Most of the time we know the difference between right and wrong but somehow we ignore it and act based on our instincts. If we could have more control on the process of choosing, most of the time we would move on the right path. The power of will, positivity, belief, perception and dream would be the fundamental forces to bring the desired transformation in your life.

About Author

Anshuman is an author and knowledge creator who has transformed the lives and work of people from every continent. His groundbreaking ideas in Thinking, Communication, Personality and Storytelling are revolutionary, simple and effective.

His belief in simplicity has created powerful solutions that can be used by everyone effortlessly.

Experience the free material from following links:

https://direct.me/anshuman

www.ingramcontent.com/pod-product-compliance
Lightning Source LLC
Chambersburg PA
CBHW051154130726
47988CB00005B/2123